Man-Made Disasters

Toxic Waste

Chemical Spills in Our World

August Greeley

Rigby

Toxic Waste: Chemical Spills in Our World
Copyright © 2002 by Rosen Book Works, Inc.

On Deck™ Reading Libraries
Published by Rigby
a division of Reed Elsevier Inc.
1000 Hart Road
Barrington, IL 60010-2627
www.rigby.com

Book Design: Christopher Logan
Text: August Greeley
Photo Credits: Cover © Peter Turnley/Corbis; pp. 4–5 © Richard Hamilton Smith/Corbis; p. 5 (inset) © James P. Blair/National Geographic Image Collection; pp. 6, 9 (top), 11, 12 (maps and illustrations) Christopher Logan; pp. 6, 12, 17 (globe logo) © PhotoDisc; p. 7 © AP/Wide World Photos/Effingham Daily News; pp. 8–9, 14, 17 © AP/Wide World Photos; p. 10 © Chris Rainier/Corbis; pp. 10 (inset), 16 © Reuters NewMedia Inc./Corbis; pp. 13, 15 (top and bottom) © AFP/Corbis; pp. 18–19 © Midwest Treaty Network, www.treatyland.com; p. 20 © Joseph Sohm, ChromoSohm Inc./Corbis; p. 21 © Todd Gipstein/Corbis

On Deck™ is a trademark of Reed Elsevier Inc.

07 06 05 04 03 02
10 9 8 7 6 5 4 3 2 1

Printed in the United States of America

ISBN 0-7578-2458-7

Contents

Chemicals in Our World

People use chemicals to make life better and easier. Some chemicals help plants grow faster. Others keep bugs off of crops. Some of these chemicals are toxic, or poisonous. When used carefully, toxic chemicals can be very helpful.

This plane sprays chemicals on farm crops. If not used carefully, chemicals can pollute the air, land, and water.

However, when toxic chemicals get into the water, land, or air, they can harm the earth. The most toxic chemical spills can kill plants, animals, and even humans!

The waste from a chemical plant in Russia polluted the air and water for miles.

Each year, there are hundreds of harmful chemical spills around the world. Spills can happen for many reasons. Sometimes, ships, trucks, and trains carrying the chemicals crash. Other times, parts of factories may break down, allowing the chemicals inside to spill outside.

Check It Out

One-third of Taiwan's rice crop is poisoned with chemicals, such as mercury and arsenic.

Russia

China

India

TAIWAN

Many chemical spills happen when the chemicals are being moved from place to place. Chemicals were spilled in this train accident.

A chemical spill does not take long to harm living things. A spill can quickly poison small plants and animals. These plants and animals may be eaten by other animals. The toxic chemicals in the plants or animals can harm the creatures that eat them. A single spill can harm or kill thousands of living things.

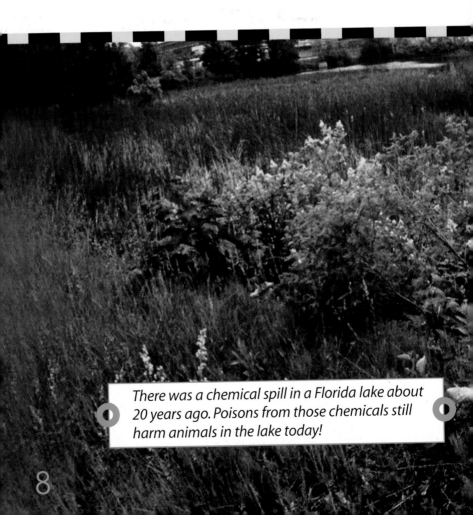

There was a chemical spill in a Florida lake about 20 years ago. Poisons from those chemicals still harm animals in the lake today!

A Lake's Food Chain

4 Birds and people eat big fish.

3 Big fish eat little fish.

2 Little fish eat algae.

1 Algae

The toxic chemicals that are taken in by algae are passed on to others in the food chain.

WARNING
Chemicals in Silver Lake may be harmful to humans

The Community Right to Know Law

In 1984, there was a huge chemical spill in India. It killed 3,000 people and 100,000 others were hurt. Two years later, the Community Right to Know Law was passed in the United States.

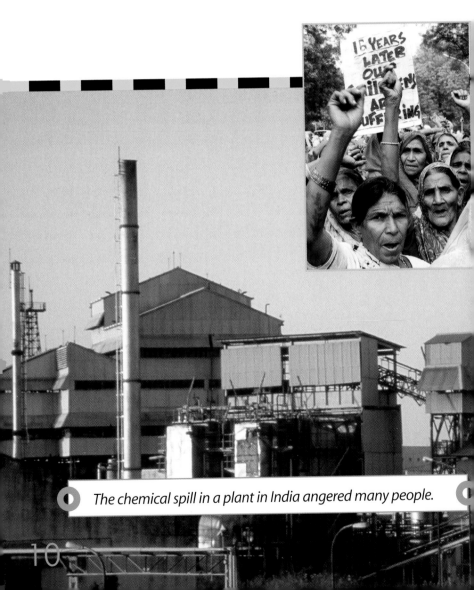

The chemical spill in a plant in India angered many people.

The law says that companies must tell the public what chemicals are being used in their factories. Every year, companies must also report the amount of toxic chemicals that they are letting out into the air, land, and water.

Chemical Spill in Romania

Since the Community Right to Know Law was passed, people have become more aware of the dangers of chemical spills. These toxic spills are still a problem, though.

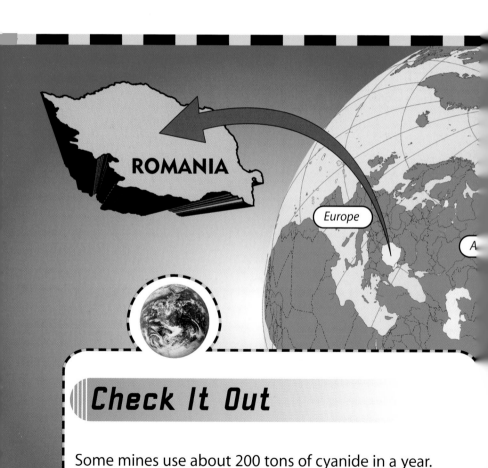

ROMANIA

Europe

Check It Out

Some mines use about 200 tons of cyanide in a year.

One very big spill happened recently. A gold mining company in Romania used a chemical called cyanide to separate gold from ordinary rock. The mining company had built a dam to keep the cyanide out of the surrounding land and water.

The owners of the mine in Romania did not tell people about the spill for 24 hours.

On January 30, 2000, heavy snowfall caused the dam to overflow. Cyanide spilled into a nearby stream. The polluted water flowed quickly from the stream in Romania into Hungary's second-largest river, the Tisza.

Before the spill, the Tisza River was one of Europe's cleanest rivers!

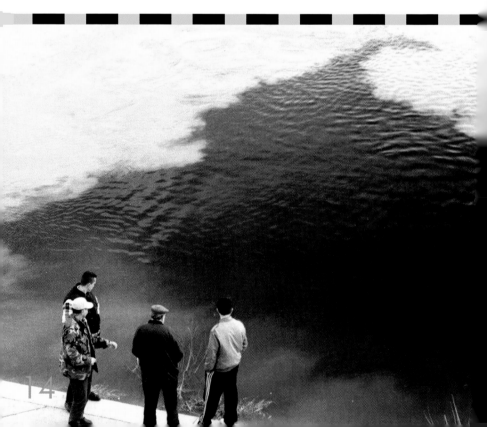

Many living things in the river, including bacteria, birds, and otters, were killed. More than 1,200 tons of fish died from this man-made disaster.

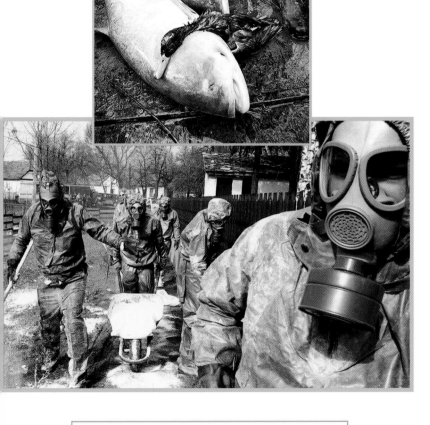

Many people worked to clean up the cyanide spill in the Tisza River.

People quickly pulled the dead fish from the Tisza River. They did not want other animals to eat the poisoned fish. About 15,000 fishermen lost their jobs because the river was so polluted.

About 26.2 million gallons of cyanide and polluted water were spilled into the Tisza River. It may take more than 10 years before fish can live in the river again.

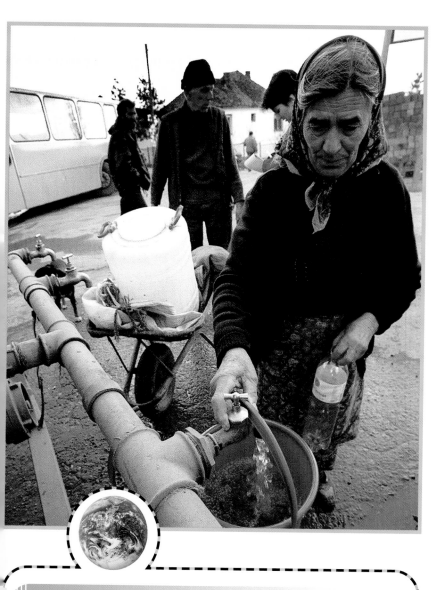

Check It Out

Poison from the chemical spill in the Tisza River left 2.5 million Hungarians without water to drink!

Some important lessons have been learned from the spill in Romania. People who lived in Wisconsin saw on TV what happened in Hungary.

They got their state government to pass a law saying that cyanide cannot be used in Wisconsin mines.

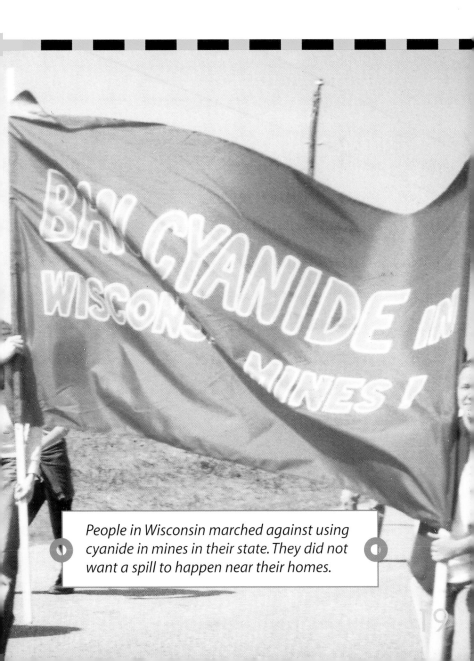

People in Wisconsin marched against using cyanide in mines in their state. They did not want a spill to happen near their homes.

Working Together

Businesses that make and use toxic chemicals are working with their communities and governments. They are trying to make chemicals that are less harmful to the earth. They are also doing everything they can to prevent toxic spills and keep the earth safe.

Toxic chemicals must be gotten rid of safely so that they do not pollute Earth.

On Earth Day, many people gather in Washington, D.C. They want to let their leaders know how they feel about harmful chemicals.

Glossary

algae (**al**-jee) small plants without stems or leaves that are found in water

arsenic (**ahr**-suh-nihk) a very poisonous chemical that is sometimes used to kill bugs and weeds

bacteria (bak-**tihr**-ee-uh) very tiny living things; some can be useful, while others cause sickness

chemical (**kehm**-uh-kuhl) a substance that is made of elements such as carbon and oxygen

chemical spill (**kehm**-uh-kuhl **spihl**) when toxic matter harms land, water, or living things

cyanide (**sy**-uh-nyd) a poisonous metal salt used in mining and in the making of plastics and bug sprays

disaster (duh-**zas**-tuhr) a sudden event that causes great loss or harm

mercury (**mer**-kyuhr-ee) a silver-white element that is poisonous

poisonous (**poi**-zn-uhs) deadly

pollute (puh-**loot**) to make the environment dirty with man-made waste

toxic (**tahk**-sihk) harmful or poisonous

Resources

Books

Chattanooga Sludge: Cleaning Toxic Sludge from Chattanooga Creek
by Molly Bang
Harcourt (1996)

Love Canal: Toxic Waste Tragedy
by Victoria Sherrow
Enslow Publishers, Inc. (2001)

Web Site

Environmental Protection Agency:
Superfund for Kids
http://www.epa.gov/superfund/kids/index.htm

Index